small plates

small plates

Annie Rigg

photography by Steve Baxter

RYLAND
PETERS
& SMALL
LONDON NEW YORK

To Céline and Iona,
the dream team

Senior Designer Iona Hoyle
Senior Editor Céline Hughes
Production Toby Marshall
Art Director Leslie Harrington
Publishing Director Alison Starling

Prop Stylist Róisín Nield
Indexer Hilary Bird

First published in 2011
by Ryland Peters & Small
20–21 Jockey's Fields
London WC1R 4BW
and
519 Broadway, 5th Floor
New York, NY 10012

www.rylandpeters.com

author's acknowledgements

A huge thank you to Steve and Róisín for
their beautiful pictures and props.

Text © Annie Rigg 2011
Design and photographs
© Ryland Peters & Small 2011

Printed in China

10 9 8 7 6 5 4 3 2 1

ISBN: 978-1-84975-134-6

A CIP record for this book is available from
the British Library.

**Library of Congress Cataloging-in-
Publication Data**

Rigg, Annie.
 Small plates / Annie Rigg ; photography by
Steve Baxter.
    p. cm.
 Includes index.
 ISBN 978-1-84975-134-6
 1. Appetizers. I. Title.
 TX740.R48 2011
 641.8'12--dc23
                                    2011014399

notes

• All spoon measurements are level, unless
otherwise specified.
• Ovens should be preheated to the
specified temperature. Recipes in this book
were tested using a regular oven. If using a
fan-assisted/convection oven, follow the
manufacturer's instructions for adjusting
temperatures.
• All eggs are medium, unless otherwise
specified. Recipes containing raw or partially
cooked egg, or raw fish or shellfish, should
not be served to the very young, very old,
anyone with a compromised immune system
or pregnant women.

contents

food for family & friends

The Spanish have tapas, the Chinese have dim sum, and meze with its little dishes of salads, dips and breads is a popular way of eating in the Middle East and the Mediterranean. What do all these cuisines have in common? They are all made up of a selection of dishes that are shared in a more communal, laid-back way of eating and entertaining.

I love food, trying new recipes and flavours, and I am a naturally greedy person. Often, I have trouble choosing just two courses from a restaurant menu and wish that I could order if not everything on the menu, then at least three or four different things to try. So the solution to this dilemma is to share smaller plates of food with my dining companions. This is fast becoming a trend in some restaurants where, rather than ordering a first course and a main course, you pick and choose from a variety of smaller plates. This book is a collection of recipes that allows you to do just this at home.

Most of the recipes here serve four people as part of a menu when served with one or two other dishes. This allows you to put together an interesting combination of flavours, tastes and textures that work well together. When you're choosing your selection of small plates, it's a good idea to group regional dishes together to avoid any major flavour clashes – Japanese sashimi just wouldn't be right with Spanish albondigas, for example. I try to aim for one spicy offering, one dish that is served cold or at room temperature, and one vegetarian option.

Most of the recipes can be partially or fully prepared in advance and reheated, assembled or garnished just before serving, allowing you, the cook, time to spend with your guests rather than being a slave to the kitchen.

As this is a more casual approach to eating, you can be a little more playful and creative with your presentation, too. Sharing means that you don't necessarily have to follow convention. Large platters can be simply served with a handful of cutlery in the middle of the table, allowing everyone to tuck in without the need for stacks of dinner plates for every course – which in turn is easy on the washing up!

Embrace this modern, sociable and fun way of eating. It marks the end of food envy and the start of endlessly satisfying grazing!

meat

A delicious combination of sweet, tender-cooked onions, salty pancetta and tangy crème fraîche, all gently infused with thyme and cooked on a buttery puff pastry base. Serve simply with a peppery rocket/arugula salad.

creamy pancetta & onion tart

1 tablespoon olive oil
170 g/5½ oz. diced pancetta
3 onions, sliced
1 fat garlic clove, crushed
1 teaspoon (caster) sugar
2 sprigs of fresh thyme
375 g/12½ oz. all-butter puff pastry dough
250 g/1 cup crème fraîche
sea salt and freshly ground black pepper

2 solid baking sheets

serves 4

Preheat the oven to 200°C (400°F) Gas 6 and place one of the baking sheets on the middle shelf to heat up.

Heat the olive oil in a large frying pan over medium heat, add the pancetta and cook until crisp. Remove from the pan with a slotted spoon and drain on kitchen paper/paper towels. Add the sliced onions to the pan and cook for about 10 minutes, stirring occasionally until they start to colour. Add the garlic, sugar and leaves from the thyme sprig and cook for a further minute to caramelize the onions. Remove from the heat, stir in the pancetta and let cool slightly.

Roll out the puff pastry dough on a lightly floured work surface. Keep rolling until it's big enough to trim into a rectangle about 30 x 20 cm/12 x 8 inches. Using the tip of the knife, score a border 2 cm/1 inch from the edge without cutting all the way through the dough. Carefully lift the dough onto the second baking sheet and slide into the preheated oven on top of the hot baking sheet. Cook for 7 minutes, then remove from the oven.

Season the crème fraîche with salt and pepper and spread half of it over the tart base. Season the onion and pancetta mixture with salt and pepper too and spread over the crème fraîche. Dot the remaining crème fraîche over the filling and return to the oven for a further 20 minutes, or until the pastry is golden and the filling is bubbling.

Serve hot or warm, cut into individual portions.

This is my take on the classic melon and prosciutto di Parma combination, but with the addition of creamy, dreamy buffalo mozzarella and ripe, juicy figs. Arrange all the ingredients beautifully on a platter and let everyone tuck in.

melon, fig, prosciutto di parma & buffalo mozzarella salad

½ canteloupe or charentais melon
½ galia or honeydew melon
4 fresh, ripe figs
12 slices of prosciutto di Parma
1 ball of buffalo mozzarella
small handful of fresh mint leaves
small handful of fresh basil leaves
freshly ground black pepper
aromatic extra virgin olive oil, to drizzle

serves 4–6

Carefully scoop the seeds out of the melons. Cut each melon into delicate wedges and cut away the skin. Arrange the melon wedges on a serving platter.

Cut the figs into halves or quarters and add to the platter.

Roughly tear the prosciutto and place next to the fruit.

Drain the mozzarella, tear into large pieces and add to the platter.

Scatter the mint and basil leaves over everything, season with black pepper, drizzle with olive oil and serve immediately with extra olive oil for those who want more.

Marinating chicken in buttermilk tenderizes the meat and makes these little chicken nuggets really juicy. Serve with chilli-spiced potato wedges and creamy coleslaw.

spiced fried chicken

3 skinless chicken breasts
150 ml/⅔ cup buttermilk
100 g/¾ cup plain/all-purpose flour
1 generous teaspoon baking powder
1 generous teaspoon sea salt flakes
½ teaspoon ground cayenne pepper
½ teaspoon Spanish smoked paprika
¼ teaspoon ground coriander
¼ teaspoon garlic powder
a pinch of ground allspice
½ teaspoon dried oregano
freshly ground black pepper
sunflower oil, for frying

serves 4

Cut each chicken breast into 5 or 6 strips. Place in a ceramic dish and coat with the buttermilk. Cover with clingfilm/plastic wrap and chill for at least 2 hours.

Remove the chicken from the buttermilk and pat off any excess with kitchen paper/paper towels. Combine the flour, baking powder, salt flakes, spices, oregano and some black pepper in a bowl. Toss the chicken pieces in the seasoned flour and set aside on baking parchment for 10 minutes.

Pour 3–4 tablespoons sunflower oil in a frying pan. Set over medium heat and add one-third of the chicken pieces. Cook until golden and crispy. Drain on kitchen paper/paper towels and repeat with the remaining 2 batches of chicken.

This is the perfect sharing dish – just put the terrine in the middle of the table with a jar of the relish, a stack of warm toasted brioche, a pile of plates and a bundle of knives and let everyone dig in. The parfait and relish can be made 2–3 days ahead of time.

chicken liver parfait
with fig relish & toasted brioche

250 g/2 sticks unsalted butter

3 shallots, sliced

2 sprigs of fresh thyme

2 garlic cloves, crushed

fresh grating of nutmeg

4 tablespoons port or Madeira

1 tablespoon olive oil

500 g/1 lb. chicken livers, trimmed

sea salt and freshly ground black pepper

toasted brioche, to serve

fig relish

125 g/4 oz. ready-to-eat dried figs, roughly chopped

50 g/⅓ cup pitted dates, roughly chopped

1 shallot, sliced

1 small eating apple, peeled, cored and finely diced

2 tablespoons light muscovado sugar

125 ml/½ cup white wine vinegar or cider vinegar

1 teaspoon grated orange zest

1 cinnamon stick

1 fresh or dried bay leaf

a pâté terrine or serving dish

serves 4–6

Melt 2 tablespoons of the butter in a small saucepan, add the shallots and half the leaves from the thyme sprigs, and cook over low–medium heat until the shallots are soft but not coloured. Add the garlic and nutmeg and continue to cook for another minute. Add the port and cook until almost all the liquid has evaporated. Remove from the heat.

Heat the oil in a large frying pan and add half the chicken livers. Cook over medium–high heat for a couple of minutes on each side until they are just cooked through but still pink in the middle. Tip the livers and the onion mixture into a food processor. Cook the remainder of the chicken livers in the same pan, then add to the food processor. Blend until smooth. Cut 175 g/1½ sticks of the butter into small pieces and gradually add to the mixture with the motor running. Push the mixture through a fine-mesh sieve into a bowl and season well with salt and black pepper.

Spoon the parfait into the terrine or serving dish and spread level. Gently melt the remaining butter, remove from the heat and leave for 2 or 3 minutes to allow the butter to separate from the whey. Leave the cloudy whey on the bottom and spoon the golden melted butter from the top onto the parfait to cover it. Scatter the remaining thyme leaves over the top and allow to set and cool before chilling.

To make the fig relish, tip all the ingredients into a medium saucepan. Cook over low heat for about 25 minutes, or until tender and jammy. Remove the cinnamon stick and bay leaf, season and let cool before serving with the parfait and some slices of toasted brioche.

A light and tangy, herb-loaded salad topped with rare, chargrilled beef. Thai basil is found in most Asian supermarkets but if you can't get it, add more coriander/cilantro and mint. You can also use cooked tiger prawns/jumbo shrimp in place of the beef.

thai-style beef salad

½ tablespoon sunflower oil

350 g/12 oz. lean rump steak/ beef top round

8 baby corn (optional)

100 g/3½ oz. mange tout/snow peas or sugar snap peas

1 red onion

2 heads baby gem or baby romaine lettuce

handful of beansprouts

1 tablespoon fresh mint leaves

1 tablespoon fresh coriander/cilantro leaves

1 tablespoon fresh Thai basil leaves

2 tablespoons chopped roasted peanuts

dressing

1 tablespoon palm sugar (jaggery) or brown sugar

1 large fresh red chilli, finely chopped

2 teaspoons grated fresh ginger

1 garlic clove, crushed

2 tablespoons fish sauce

freshly squeezed juice of 1 lime

1 teaspoon soy sauce

serves 4

Heat a ridged stovetop griddle/grill pan until smoking hot. Rub the oil all over the steak and cook for 2–3 minutes on each side, depending on the thickness and how well cooked you like your steak. Medium-rare would be my preference for this salad. Remove the steak from the pan and set aside while you prepare the remaining ingredients.

Bring a small pan of salted water to the boil. Add the baby corn (if using) and cook for 1 minute before adding the mange tout/snow peas. Cook for a further minute, then drain and refresh under cold running water. Slice the baby corn and mange tout/snow peas on the diagonal.

Peel and finely slice the red onion. Shred the lettuce and arrange on a platter. Scatter the onion, baby corn, mange tout and beansprouts over the lettuce.

To make the dressing, whisk together all the ingredients until smooth, then pour it over the salad.

Slice the steak into strips, arrange on the salad, scatter the herbs and chopped peanuts over the top and serve immediately.

All the work for this dish can be done ahead of time: the ragù and tomato sauce can be made, the pasta cooked and filled, and the dish completely assembled. Sprinkle the cheese over the top and heat in a moderate oven when needed.

baked large pasta shells
with ragù & tomato sauce

1 onion, finely chopped

2 tablespoons olive oil

2 fat garlic cloves, crushed

40 g/1½ oz. pancetta, finely chopped

300 g/10 oz. lean minced/ground beef

2 tablespoons tomato paste

125 ml/½ cup red wine

400 g/14 oz. canned chopped tomatoes

225 ml/1 cup vegetable stock

½ teaspoon dried oregano

1 teaspoon (caster) sugar

200 g/6½ oz. conchiglioni rigati pasta (large pasta shells)

2 tablespoons freshly grated Parmesan

1 generous tablespoon freshly grated cheddar

sea salt and freshly ground black pepper

fresh basil leaves, to serve

medium ovenproof dish

serves 4

For the ragù, gently fry half the onion in a saucepan with half the oil. Add half the garlic and all the pancetta and continue to cook for a couple of minutes until tender but not coloured. Add the beef and brown quickly. Add half the tomato paste and all the wine and cook for 30 seconds, then add half the chopped tomatoes and half the stock. Bring to the boil, then reduce the heat to a very gentle simmer and cook for about 1 hour, or until the beef is tender and the sauce thick.

To make the tomato sauce, heat the remaining oil in another pan, add the remaining onion and fry gently until tender. Add the remaining garlic, cook for 30 seconds, then add the remaining tomato paste, chopped tomatoes, stock and oregano. Bring to the boil, reduce the heat to a gentle simmer and cook for about 30 minutes, or until reduced slightly. Taste and add a pinch of sugar if needed and plenty of salt and black pepper.

Preheat the oven to 190°C (375°F) Gas 5.

Cook the pasta in a large pan of salted water until al dente, following the package instructions. Drain, refresh under cold running water, then drain well again.

Pour the tomato sauce into an ovenproof dish. Fill each pasta shell with the ragù and arrange over the tomato sauce. Scatter a mixture of grated Parmesan and cheddar all over the pasta and bake in the preheated oven for about 20 minutes, or until bubbling hot.

Scatter basil over the baked dish and serve immediately.

Possibly one of the easiest recipes around, as there is very little cooking involved here. It's more of an assembling job – why not have all the fillings in bowls and allow everyone to create their own favourite quesadilla?

quesadillas
with chorizo or chicken filling

200 g/2 cups diced butternut squash
1 tablespoon olive oil
½ teaspoon Spanish smoked paprika
100 g/3½ oz. cooking chorizo, diced
8 flour tortillas
4 tablespoons refried beans
1 cooked chicken breast, shredded
1 bunch of spring onions/scallions, thinly sliced
2 tablespoons roughly chopped jalapeños
2 tablespoons freshly chopped coriander/cilantro
200 g/6½ oz. cheddar, grated
sea salt and freshly ground black pepper

serves 4

Preheat the oven to 220°C (425°F) Gas 7.

Tip the butternut squash into a roasting dish and toss in the olive oil and paprika. Season with salt and pepper and roast on the middle shelf of the preheated oven for about 15 minutes. Remove from the oven, add the chorizo and roast for another 10 minutes, or until golden brown and the squash is tender. Lightly mash the squash and let cool slightly before making the quesadillas.

Lay 2 of the tortillas out on the work surface. Spread the refried beans evenly between them, top with the shredded chicken, half the spring onions/scallions and half the jalapeños. Scatter half the coriander/cilantro and half the grated cheddar over the top and lay another tortilla on top of each one.

Lay another 2 tortillas out and spread the roasted squash and chorizo mixture evenly between them. Scatter the remaining spring onions/scallions, jalapeños, coriander/cilantro and grated cheddar over the top and lay another tortilla on top of each one.

Heat a ridged stovetop griddle/grill pan over medium heat and add the quesadillas, one at a time. Cook until golden and the cheese starts to melt. Gently flip the quesadilla over and cook the other side until golden. Cut into quarters and serve immediately.

Finger-licking good! You'll need a pile of napkins for these. Serve with Thai-style Mini Fish Cakes (page 35), Vietnamese Rice Paper Rolls (page 32) and ice-cold beers.

sticky spare ribs
with honey & soy glaze

1 kg/2 lbs. short or loin pork ribs/
country-style pork spare ribs

4 garlic cloves, crushed

2 tablespoons grated fresh ginger

4 tablespoons (clear) honey

2 tablespoons soy sauce

2 tablespoons hoisin sauce

2 tablespoons sweet chilli sauce

2 tablespoons tamarind paste

¼ teaspoon Chinese five-spice powder

large roasting dish

serves 4–6

Place the ribs in a saucepan of water, bring up to the boil and simmer for 5–10 minutes, then drain.

Mix the remaining ingredients together in a large bowl, add the ribs and stir thoroughly to coat. Let cool and allow to marinate for about 30 minutes.

Preheat the oven to 190°C (375°F) Gas 5.

Tip the ribs and marinade into a large roasting dish, cover with foil and cook on the middle shelf of the preheated oven for about 20 minutes. Remove the foil, turn the ribs over, basting them with the marinade, and cook for another 20 minutes until sticky and browned all over. Allow to rest for a couple of minutes before serving with plenty of napkins.

As well as the suggestions given below, you could serve these mini pizzas with any variety of toppings. One of my favourites is sautéed onions, dolcelatte and a handful of wild rocket/arugula added just before serving.

pizzette
with assorted meaty & veggie toppings

pizza dough
½ x 7-g sachet/package or 1½ level
teaspoons fast-action/instant dried yeast
250 g/2 cups plain/all-purpose flour
½ teaspoon fine sea salt
5 tablespoons olive oil
175 ml/⅔ cup hand-hot water

toppings
1 small aubergine/eggplant, thinly sliced
1 onion, thinly sliced
pinch of fresh thyme leaves
4 generous teaspoons sun-dried
tomato paste
75 g/½ cup cherry tomatoes, quartered
125 g/4 oz. dolcelatte or gorgonzola,
crumbled
8 slices of pepperoni
handful of black olives
100 g/3½ oz. mozzarella, diced
2 teaspoons basil pesto
2 canned artichoke hearts, sliced
2 tablespoons semi-dried tomatoes
handful of wild rocket/arugula
sea salt and freshly ground black pepper
fresh basil leaves, to garnish

solid baking sheet

makes 4 mini pizzas

To make the pizza dough, mix together the flour, yeast and salt in a large bowl. Add 2 tablespoons of the olive oil and the water and mix to a soft dough. Lightly dust the work surface with flour, tip the dough out of the bowl and knead for 5 minutes, or until smooth and elastic. Shape the dough into a neat, smooth ball, return to the bowl and cover with clingfilm/plastic wrap. Leave in a warm place for 1 hour, or until doubled in size.

Heat 2 tablespoons of the oil in a frying pan and fry the aubergine/eggplant on both sides until golden, then remove from the heat. In another pan, heat the remaining olive oil and gently fry the onion until very tender and just starting to turn golden. Add the thyme and remove from the heat.

Preheat the oven to 230°C (450°F) Gas 8.

Divide the dough into 4 evenly sized pieces and shape each piece into a pizza about 15 cm/6 inches in diameter. Place on a solid baking sheet, then spread sun-dried tomato paste over 2 of the pizzas. Top one pizza with the aubergine/eggplant slices, cherry tomatoes and half the crumbled dolcelatte. Top the other pizza with pepperoni, olives and half the diced mozzarella.

For the third pizza, spread the basil pesto over the base and arrange the artichoke hearts and semi-dried tomatoes on top. Scatter the remaining mozzarella over it. Garnish with basil leaves. Top the last pizza with the sautéed onions and remaining dolcelatte. Season all the pizzas well with salt and pepper and cook on the top shelf of the preheated oven for about 5 minutes, or until golden. Top the onion pizza with the rocket/arugula and serve immediately.

You can prepare these flavourful meatballs and their spiced tomato sauce ahead and reheat in a covered casserole dish either in a moderate oven or on the stovetop. They actually taste better if you make them 24 hours in advance.

albóndigas
with spiced tomato sauce

3 tablespoons olive oil
2 onions, finely chopped
3 fat garlic cloves, crushed
1 teaspoon dried oregano
½ teaspoon crushed dried chillies
½ teaspoon ground cumin
200 ml/¾ cup red wine
400-g/14-oz. can chopped tomatoes
1 strip of orange peel
1 teaspoon (caster) sugar
sea salt and freshly ground black pepper

albóndigas

200 g/6½ oz. good-quality pork sausages
350 g/12 oz. lean minced/ground beef
1 teaspoon Spanish smoked paprika
½ teaspoon ground cumin
2 generous tablespoons freshly chopped
flat-leaf parsley, plus extra to garnish
1 small egg, beaten
3 tablespoons fresh white breadcrumbs
1 tablespoon milk

serves 4–6

Heat 2 tablespoons of the oil in a frying pan and fry the onions until soft but not coloured. Add the garlic and oregano and continue to cook for 1 minute. Scoop half the onions into a bowl and let cool.

Add the crushed dried chillies and ground cumin to the pan and cook for 30 seconds. Add the red wine, chopped tomatoes and orange peel and cook gently for about 30 minutes, or until the sauce has thickened slightly. Season well with salt, pepper and the sugar, to balance the flavours. Remove from the heat and set aside while you prepare the albóndigas.

To make the albóndigas, remove the skin from the sausages and add the meat to the cooled, cooked onions along with the beef, paprika, ground cumin, parsley, egg, breadcrumbs and milk. Using your hands, mix until combined, season well with salt and pepper, then roll into 20 walnut-sized balls.

Heat the remaining oil in a large frying pan and brown the albóndigas in batches, adding more oil if necessary.

Add the albóndigas to the spiced tomato sauce and cook gently over low heat for a further 30 minutes. Sprinkle more chopped parsley over the top before serving.

This dish can be served alongside the Albóndigas (page 26) and Patatas Bravas (page 54). Padrón peppers are small, strongly flavoured green peppers that are pan fried, seasoned with sea salt and eaten whole. Look for them in Spanish delis.

chorizo & olives in red wine
with padrón peppers

150 g/5 oz. cooking chorizo
1 garlic clove, peeled and smashed
1 sprig of fresh thyme
150 ml/⅔ cup red wine
1 tablespoon sherry vinegar or balsamic vinegar
2 tablespoons mixed olives in olive oil, plus 1 tablespoon oil from the jar
1 tablespoon freshly chopped flat-leaf parsley
150 g/5 oz. Padrón peppers, or green (bell) peppers (seeds removed), sliced
sea salt flakes

serves 4

Cut the chorizo into bite-size chunks. Heat a frying pan over medium heat, add the chorizo and cook until it starts to brown and crisp at the edges. Add the smashed garlic, leaves from the thyme sprig and red wine to the pan and continue to cook over medium heat until the red wine has reduced by half. Add the vinegar and cook for 30 seconds or so. Add the olives and chopped parsley.

Meanwhile, heat the tablespoon of olive oil from the jar of olives in another pan and add the whole Padrón peppers. Cook over medium heat until hot and starting to brown at the edges. Season with salt flakes and serve with the chorizo.

seafood

Often the classic retro dishes are the best, and this is one such example. Use a selection of different prawns/shrimp to make this a more sophisticated number. If you're feeling glam, add some cooked chopped lobster or crayfish tails to the mix.

seafood cocktails

12 cherry tomatoes
4 spring onions/scallions, trimmed
1 fresh red chilli
1 garlic clove, crushed
freshly squeezed juice of 1 lime
400 g/14 oz. cooked and peeled prawns/shrimp in assorted sizes
2 tablespoons freshly chopped coriander/cilantro
a few drops of Tabasco sauce
1 ripe avocado
½ iceberg lettuce, shredded
sea salt and freshly ground black pepper
lime wedges, to serve

4–6 individual dishes or glasses

serves 4–6

Roughly chop the tomatoes and finely slice the spring onions/scallions. Remove the seeds from the chilli and finely chop the flesh. Put these chopped ingredients in a bowl with the crushed garlic and freshly squeezed lime juice and mix well. Add the prawns/shrimp, chopped coriander/cilantro, a shake of Tabasco sauce and season well with salt and black pepper.

Set aside to marinate for 10 minutes.

Peel and dice the avocado and gently stir into the prawn/shrimp mixture. Arrange a handful of shredded lettuce in each dish, spoon the prawn/shrimp mixture over the top and serve immediately with extra lime wedges.

You'll find rice paper wrappers in Asian supermarkets – they are often called 'banh trang' and should not be confused with wonton wrappers. If you don't have time to make the dipping sauce, serve these light, fresh, herb-filled rolls with hoisin sauce.

vietnamese rice paper rolls

40 g/1½ oz. rice vermicelli noodles
¼ cucumber, peeled
1 carrot, peeled
1 head baby gem or baby romaine lettuce
handful of beansprouts
150 g/5 oz. cooked king prawns/
jumbo shrimp
12 rice paper wrappers, 16 cm/6 inches
2 tablespoons fresh mint leaves
2 tablespoons fresh coriander/cilantro leaves
12 fresh chives

dipping sauce
1 hot fresh red chilli
1 fat garlic clove
1 generous tablespoon palm sugar (jaggery)
or brown sugar
freshly squeezed juice of 1 lime
½ tablespoon fish sauce
½ tablespoon rice wine vinegar
1 tablespoon chopped salted peanuts

serves 4–6

Prepare the dipping sauce first. Remove the seeds from the chilli and finely chop the flesh. Roughly chop the garlic and pound to a paste using a pestle and mortar. Add the remaining ingredients and mix until smooth. Taste and add more fish sauce or sugar to balance the flavours. Set aside while you prepare the rolls.

Have all the ingredients for the rolls lined up on a tray. Pour boiling water over the rice noodles in a bowl and let soak for 5 minutes. Cut the cucumber and carrot into fine matchsticks. Finely shred the lettuce and cut the prawns/shrimp in half lengthways to make them thinner. Drain the noodles well on kitchen paper/paper towels.

Take one rice paper wrapper at a time and soak in a bowl of warm water for 1 minute, or until soft. Very gently lift it out of the water and drain quickly on a clean tea towel. Lay the wrapper on the work surface, cut the noodles into short, equal lengths and arrange in a neat pile down the middle of the wrapper, leaving space at each end to fold the wrapper over later. Top with the shredded vegetables, the prawns/shrimp and scatter some of the herbs over the top. Fold one side of the wrapper over the length of the filling, then bring the short sides over to encase the ingredients. Tightly roll the wrapper up to form a neat cigar shape. Arrange on a plate, seam-side down.

Continue with the remaining wrappers and ingredients. Serve with the dipping sauce.

These little fish cakes can be prepared and cooked in advance, then reheated, covered with foil, in a moderate oven. Serve alongside Vietnamese Rice Paper Rolls (page 32) and Sticky Spare Ribs (page 22), and even a bowl of sticky jasmine or egg fried rice.

thai-style mini fish cakes
with cucumber & peanut dipping sauce

125 g/4 oz. skinless, boneless cod or other white fish

150 g/5 oz. raw peeled and deveined prawns/shrimp

100 g/1 cup grated fresh coconut

1 fresh red chilli

4 spring onions/scallions, sliced

1 tablespoon freshly chopped coriander/cilantro

1 tablespoon Thai red curry paste

pinch of salt

2–3 tablespoons sunflower oil, for frying

lime wedges, to serve

dipping sauce

125 ml/½ cup rice wine vinegar

100 g/½ cup (caster) sugar

1 fresh red chilli, finely chopped

1 carrot

3-cm/1-inch piece of cucumber

1 tablespoon roasted peanuts

serves 2–4

Prepare the dipping sauce first. Pour the vinegar into a small saucepan, add the sugar and bring slowly to the boil to dissolve the sugar. Simmer until the syrup thickens slightly. Add the chilli, remove from the heat and let cool. Peel and finely dice the carrot. Scrape the seeds from the cucumber, discard, then finely dice the flesh. Roughly chop the peanuts. Add everything to the cooled chilli syrup.

To make the fish cakes, cut the fish into large chunks and place in a food processor with the prawns/shrimp and coconut. Whizz until combined and nearly smooth. Remove the seeds from the chilli and finely chop the flesh. Tip into a bowl with the blended fish mixture, spring onions/scallions, coriander/cilantro, curry paste and salt. Mix well. Divide the mixture into 8–10 evenly sized portions and, using wet hands, shape into patties.

Heat the oil in a frying pan over medium heat and fry the fish cakes in 2 or 3 batches until golden brown, about 2 minutes on each side. Drain on kitchen paper/paper towels and serve with lime wedges and the dipping sauce.

I've chosen salmon and tuna for this pretty sashimi with ginger soy dressing and micro herb garnish. Ask your fishmonger for the very best, freshest fish he has to offer. If you prefer, you can sear the fish quickly in a smoking-hot frying pan.

mixed sashimi
with ginger soy dressing & micro herbs

250 g/8 oz. sushi-grade tuna fillet
250 g/8 oz. skinless salmon fillet, pin bones removed
5-cm/2-inch piece of mooli/daikon radish
4 red-skinned radishes, trimmed
4 spring onions/scallions, trimmed
1 tablespoon pickled ginger
micro herbs, baby rocket/arugula, or fresh coriander/cilantro

ginger soy dressing
½ fresh red chilli, finely chopped
½–1 teaspoon wasabi paste
2 tablespoons soy sauce
freshly squeezed juice of ½ lime

serves 4

Cut the fish into thin slices and arrange on a platter.

Peel and cut the mooli into fine matchsticks. Cut the radishes into fine matchsticks. Thinly slice the spring onions/scallions. Mix the mooli/daikon, radishes and spring onions/scallions together and add to the platter. Add the pickled ginger, too.

To make the ginger soy dressing, mix together the chopped chilli, wasabi paste, soy sauce and lime juice in a little bowl.

Garnish the sashimi with the micro herbs and serve immediately with the ginger soy dressing.

Try to use small, tender baby squid rings with tentacles for this recipe and serve as part of a meal with the Assorted Focaccia Crostini (page 58) or Albóndigas (page 26).

crispy calamari
with butter beans & chorizo

2 tablespoons olive oil
1 onion, thinly sliced
1 garlic clove, crushed
½ teaspoon cumin seeds, lightly crushed
pinch of crushed dried chillies
½ teaspoon dried oregano
100 g/3½ oz. cooking chorizo, diced
200-g/6½-oz. can chopped tomatoes
400-g/14-oz. can butter beans, drained
2 tablespoons freshly chopped
flat-leaf parsley
250 g/8 oz. small squid tubes
2 tablespoons plain/all-purpose flour
sugar, for seasoning (optional)
sea salt and freshly ground black pepper

serves 4

Heat half the oil in a medium saucepan, add the onion and cook for 4–5 minutes until tender but not coloured. Add the garlic, cumin, chillies and oregano and continue to cook for another minute. Add the diced chorizo and cook until lightly browned and the onions have started to caramelize.

Add the chopped tomatoes and drained beans and simmer for about 20 minutes, or until thick. Add the parsley and season with salt and black pepper, plus a pinch of sugar if the sauce needs it to balance the tomatoes.

Cut the squid into 1-cm/½-inch thick rings, pat dry on kitchen paper/paper towels and toss in seasoned flour. Heat the remaining oil in a large frying pan, and when it's smoking hot, add half the prepared squid. Cook for 2–3 minutes until golden brown and cooked through. Remove from the pan and cook the remaining squid. Spoon the calamari on top of the chorizo and butter-bean mixture and serve immediately.

My take on fancy fish and chips. For this recipe I have fried the breadcrumbs until golden in a little olive oil and butter – this way the fish can be baked in the oven rather than deep-fried. Serve with oven-cooked fries, ketchup and tartare sauce.

sole goujons

2 tablespoons olive oil
2 tablespoons unsalted butter
200 g/4 cups fresh, fine breadcrumbs
1 tablespoon freshly chopped flat-leaf parsley
2 teaspoons freshly chopped thyme
finely grated zest of 1 unwaxed lemon
1 teaspoon Spanish smoked paprika
450 g/1 lb. skinless sole fillets
4 tablespoons plain/all-purpose flour
2 eggs, beaten
sea salt and freshly ground black pepper

to serve
tomato ketchup
tartare sauce
oven-cooked french fries
lemon wedges

baking sheet, lined with baking parchment

serves 4

Preheat the oven to 220°C (425°F) Gas 7.

Heat the oil and butter in a large frying pan, add the breadcrumbs and, stirring constantly, cook until golden. Tip the crumbs into a large bowl, add the chopped herbs, lemon zest and paprika and season well with salt and black pepper. Let cool.

Cut each sole fillet into strips roughly 2–3 cm/1 inch wide.

Tip the flour into one shallow dish and the beaten eggs into another. Taking one piece of fish at a time, coat it first in the flour, then the beaten eggs, then the golden breadcrumbs. Arrange the goujons on the prepared baking sheet and bake in the preheated oven for about 10 minutes, or until cooked through.

Serve immediately with tomato ketchup, tartare sauce, oven-cooked french fries and lemon wedges.

A super-tasty and super-easy dish to knock out in no time at all, and that can be served hot or warm. I have used one large piece of salmon but you could just as easily use 4 smaller pieces and serve them as individual portions.

sesame & ginger seared salmon

4–5-cm/2-inch piece of fresh ginger, peeled and grated
1 fat garlic clove, crushed
3 tablespoons soy sauce
2 tablespoons (runny) honey
1 tablespoon sesame oil
2 tablespoons rice wine vinegar
500 g/1 lb. skinless salmon fillet, pin bones removed
1 tablespoon mixed white and black sesame seeds, toasted
sea salt
steamed baby bok choy and tenderstem broccoli, to serve

sticky coconut rice
200 g/1 cup basmati rice
150 ml/⅔ cup coconut milk

baking sheet, lined with foil

serves 4

Combine the ginger, garlic, soy sauce, honey, sesame oil and vinegar in a shallow dish. Add the salmon and turn in the marinade. Cover and leave to marinate for 1 hour, turning the fish over halfway through.

To make the sticky coconut rice, put the rice in a bowl, cover with cold water and let soak for 20 minutes. Preheat the grill/broiler to medium.

Drain and rinse the rice under cold running water. Tip the rice into a medium saucepan, add the coconut milk, 300 ml/1¼ cups water and a pinch of salt. Bring to the boil and reduce the heat to a gentle simmer. Cover and cook for 10 minutes, or until tender.

Remove the salmon from the marinade (reserve the marinade), lay on the prepared baking sheet and grill/broil for about 5–7 minutes until cooked through. Meanwhile, tip the marinade into a small saucepan, add 3–4 tablespoons water and simmer gently over low heat for 2 minutes, or until thickened slightly. Strain the sauce and pour over the grilled/broiled salmon.

Scatter the toasted sesame seeds over the salmon and serve immediately with the sticky coconut rice and steamed baby bok choy and tenderstem broccoli.

veggies

These crispy nuggets of chickpeas, beans and masses of herbs are delicious served with home-made hummus, warm flatbreads and snappy pickled chilli peppers. If you'd rather not deep-fry the falafel, you can shallow-fry them in 1 cm/½ inch oil instead.

very herby falafel
with red pepper hummus & pickled chillies

200 g/1 cup dried chickpeas
100 g/1 cup shelled broad/fava beans or butter beans
2 garlic cloves, crushed
2 tablespoons freshly chopped coriander/cilantro
2 tablespoons freshly chopped flat-leaf parsley
2 tablespoons freshly chopped mint
1 shallot, finely chopped
1 teaspoon ground cumin
1 teaspoon ground coriander
½ teaspoon ground cayenne pepper
1 teaspoon bicarbonate of/baking soda
freshly squeezed juice of 1 lemon
2 tablespoons sesame seeds
sea salt and freshly ground black pepper
about 1 litre/4 cups sunflower oil, for deep-frying
toasted flatbreads and pickled mild green chilli peppers, to serve

red pepper hummus
400-g/14-oz. can chickpeas
1 tablespoon tahini
4 tablespoons fruity olive oil
1 garlic clove
1 roasted red (bell) pepper, from a jar
freshly squeezed juice of ½ lemon

makes 12

Soak the dried chickpeas overnight in a large bowl of cold water.

The next day, drain and rinse the chickpeas. Bring a saucepan of water to the boil, add half the chickpeas and cook for about 15–20 minutes, or until tender. Add the broad/fava beans and cook for a further 2 minutes. Drain and tip into the bowl of a food processor with the remaining uncooked, soaked chickpeas.

Add the garlic, chopped herbs, shallot, spices, bicarbonate of/baking soda, lemon juice and 1 teaspoon salt. Season well with black pepper and whiz until almost smooth and well combined.

Tip the mixture into a bowl and roll into 12 even-sized balls, then flatten slightly to make patties. Press the sesame seeds into both sides of each falafel.

Fill a deep-fat fryer with sunflower oil or pour oil to a depth of about 4 cm/1½ inches into a deep saucepan. Heat until a cube of bread sizzles and browns in about 5 seconds. Cook the falafel in batches of 3–4 at a time in the hot fat until golden brown. Drain on kitchen paper/paper towels.

To make the red pepper hummus, drain and rinse the canned chickpeas. Put them in the bowl of the food processor with the tahini, olive oil, garlic and red pepper and whiz until smooth. Season well with salt and black pepper and lemon juice to taste.

Serve the falafel with the red pepper hummus, toasted flatbreads, and pickled green chilli peppers.

Serve this vibrant, zingy soup chilled and in small glasses. It can be prepared and chilled in advance and garnished just before serving. Why not serve it with something rich, like Chicken Liver Parfait (page 14) or Creamy Pancetta & Onion Tart (page 8)?

minted pea soup
with frazzled prosciutto di parma

1 bunch of spring onions/scallions
1 tablespoon olive oil
1 fat garlic clove, crushed
1 potato, peeled and diced
750 ml/3 cups hot vegetable stock
300 g/3½ cups frozen peas
a big handful of rocket/arugula, roughly chopped
1 generous tablespoon freshly chopped mint
sea salt and freshly ground black pepper

to garnish
4 slices of prosciutto di Parma
1 tablespoon olive oil
pea shoots
crème fraîche or sour cream

4–6 small glasses

serves 4–6

Trim and slice the spring onions/scallions. Heat the oil in a medium saucepan, add the spring onions/scallions and garlic and cook over medium heat for a couple of minutes until tender but not coloured. Add the diced potato to the pan along with the vegetable stock. Bring to the boil, then simmer gently for about 20 minutes, or until the potato is really tender. Add the peas, rocket/arugula and mint and cook for a further 3–4 minutes.

Tip the contents of the pan into the bowl of a food processor or blender and blend until smooth. Pass the soup through a fine sieve and season with salt and black pepper. If the soup is too thick, add a little more vegetable stock.

Chill the soup until ready to serve.

To garnish, roughly tear the prosciutto into pieces. Heat the oil in a frying pan, add the prosciutto and cook until crisp. Remove from the heat and drain on kitchen paper/paper towels.

Divide the soup between 4–6 small glasses. Add a teaspoon of crème fraîche to each, top with pea shoots, crisp prosciutto and a bit of black pepper, and serve immediately.

Like focaccia, grissini are a cinch to make. They can be baked in advance and reheated to crisp up just before serving. This recipe may make more grissini than you need but you'll find yourself nibbling on them as soon as they come out of the oven.

cannellini & artichoke dip
with olive & fennel-seed grissini

grissini
375 g/3 cups (strong) white bread flour

7-g sachet/package or 3 level teaspoons fast-action/instant dried yeast

1 teaspoon fine sea salt

1 teaspoon fennel seeds, lightly crushed

225 ml/1 scant cup milk

3 tablespoons olive oil

2 tablespoons chopped green olives

2–3 teaspoons finely chopped fresh rosemary

3 tablespoons finely grated Parmesan

cannellini & artichoke dip
400-g/14-oz. can cannellini beans, drained and rinsed

4 artichoke hearts marinated in olive oil, roughly chopped, plus 2 tablespoons oil from the jar

2 tablespoons freshly chopped flat-leaf parsley

1 fat garlic clove

grated zest and freshly squeezed juice from ½ lemon

sea salt and freshly ground black pepper

2–3 solid baking sheets

serves 4–6

To make the grissini, mix together the flour, yeast, salt and fennel seeds in a large bowl. Warm the milk in a small saucepan until it is hand-hot but not boiling, stir in the olive oil, then pour into the large bowl with the dry ingredients. Mix until the dough comes together. Lightly dust the work surface with flour, tip the dough out of the bowl and knead for about 5 minutes, or until smooth and elastic. Add the chopped olives, rosemary and Parmesan and knead again until thoroughly incorporated.

Shape the dough into a neat, smooth ball, return to the bowl and cover with clingfilm/plastic wrap. Leave in a warm place for about 1 hour, or until doubled in size.

Lightly dust the work surface with flour again, tip the dough out and knead for about 1 minute. Roll the dough into a rectangle roughly 5–7 mm/¼ inch thick. Cut the dough into finger-width strips, roll each strip slightly to round off the edges and arrange on the baking sheets. Let rise for 15 minutes while you preheat the oven to 180°C (350°F) Gas 4.

Bake the grissini on the middle shelf of the preheated oven for about 10 minutes, or until golden and crisp.

To make the cannellii & artichoke dip, put all the ingredients in the bowl of a food processor and whiz until just smooth.

Serve the warm grissini immediately with the cannellini & artichoke dip.

For this recipe, use goat cheese logs that have a soft white rind. I have used rocket/ arugula here, as the peppery leaves contrast wonderfully with the creamy cheese, sweet pears and tangy pomegranate, but you could use watercress or chicory/endive.

crumbed & baked goat cheese
with herbed ciabatta croutons & winter fruit salad

1 ciabatta loaf
4 tablespoons olive oil
2 teaspoons freshly chopped thyme
2 teaspoons freshly chopped oregano
2 x 120-g goat cheese logs (with rind)
1 egg, beaten

winter fruit salad

2 red pears
2 green pears
1 pomegranate
3 handfuls of wild rocket/arugula leaves
50 g/½ cup toasted hazelnuts, roughly chopped
2 tablespoons balsamic vinegar
5 tablespoons hazelnut oil
sea salt and freshly ground black pepper

solid baking sheet

serves 4–6

Make the breadcrumbs and herbed ciabatta croutons first. Cut the ciabatta in half. Take one half, roughly chop and put in a food processor. Whiz until you get fine breadcrumbs. Heat half the oil in a frying pan, add the breadcrumbs and toast until golden. Remove from the pan and drain on kitchen paper/paper towels. If the breadcrumbs are on the chunky side, whiz them again in the food processor for another 30 seconds.

Preheat the grill/broiler to medium. Slice the remaining ciabatta into long, thin slices. Mix the remaining oil with the chopped herbs and brush over one side of the bread. Toast under the hot grill/broiler, turning over once, until golden on both sides.

Preheat the oven to 180°C (350°F) Gas 4.

Trim the ends off each goat cheese log and cut each log into 3 evenly sized pieces. Lightly dip the cheese pieces in the beaten egg, then roll in the toasted breadcrumbs to completely cover. Arrange on a baking sheet and cook in the preheated oven for about 7 minutes, or until warm and bubbling.

While the cheese is baking, make the winter fruit salad. Quarter, core and slice the pears into slim wedges. Cut the pomegranate into quarters and pick out the beautiful jewel-like seeds. Arrange the pears, pomegranate seeds and rocket/arugula on a large serving platter and scatter the chopped hazelnuts over the top.

Whisk the balsamic vinegar and hazelnut oil together and drizzle over the salad. Nestle the warm cheese over the top, tuck the herbed ciabatta croutons alongside and serve immediately.

Serve this colourful salad warm or at room temperature (rather than cold), and piled high on a beautiful bowl or platter. If you prefer, you could use feta in place of the goat cheese, and it would be delicious served with warm, freshly baked focaccia.

roasted vegetable salad
with herby goat cheese

1 tablespoon sea salt flakes

4 small–medium beetroot/beets, leaves trimmed

½ medium butternut squash, seeds removed

2 garlic cloves, unpeeled

1 large sprig of fresh thyme

4 tablespoons olive oil

1 red onion

1 red (bell) pepper

6 baby leeks, trimmed

a handful of baby leaf spinach and wild rocket/arugula

150 g/5 oz. mild soft goat cheese

2 tablespoons toasted pumpkin seeds

sea salt and freshly ground black pepper

salsa verde

2 tablespoons fresh flat-leaf parsley leaves

2 tablespoons fresh mint leaves

2 tablespoons fresh basil leaves

4 tablespoons fruity olive oil

1 teaspoon capers

1 teaspoon Dijon mustard

small roasting dish, lined with foil

serves 4–6

Preheat the oven to 170°C (325°F) Gas 3.

Sprinkle the salt flakes over the prepared roasting dish. Arrange the beetroot/beets on top and cover tightly with foil. Roast on the middle shelf of the preheated oven for about 1 hour, or until the beetroots/beets are tender when tested with the point of a small knife. Remove the foil and let cool.

Turn the oven up to 200°C (400°F) Gas 6.

Meanwhile, cut the butternut squash into 8 wedges, arrange on another baking sheet with the whole garlic cloves and the leaves from the thyme sprig. Drizzle the olive oil over the top, season with salt and pepper and roast on the top shelf of the oven for 15 minutes.

Peel and cut the red onion into 8 wedges through the root, and the red pepper into large chunks. Add these and the whole leeks to the squash and continue to cook for 20 minutes, or until tender. Remove from the oven and let cool to room temperature.

While the vegetables are roasting, prepare the salsa verde. Tip all the ingredients into the bowl of a small food processor, whiz until smooth and season with salt and black pepper.

Peel the skin from the roasted beetroot and cut into wedges. Arrange all the roasted vegetables on a serving platter with the salad leaves. Crumble the goat cheese and scatter over the top with the toasted pumpkin seeds. Drizzle the salsa verde over the salad and serve immediately.

I find it impossible to think of tapas without a plate of piquant *patatas bravas*. I've given this classic recipe a facelift and added sweet potatoes and cherry tomatoes.

patatas bravas

2 large potatoes
2 orange-fleshed sweet potatoes
4 tablespoons olive oil
1 onion, chopped
2 garlic cloves, sliced
1 teaspoon coriander seeds
1 teaspoon cumin seeds
1 teaspoon Spanish smoked paprika
big pinch of crushed dried chillies
150 g/5 oz. cherry tomatoes
sea salt and freshly ground black pepper
freshly chopped flat-leaf parsley, to garnish

serves 4

Preheat the oven to 225°C (425°F) Gas 7.

Peel and cut the large potatoes into large, bite-size chunks, tip into a saucepan of salted water and bring to the boil. Cook over medium heat for about 5–7 minutes. Drain and leave the potatoes to dry in the colander.

Peel and cut the sweet potato into chunks the same size as the other potatoes and tip into a roasting dish. Add the blanched potatoes, drizzle half the olive oil over them and roast in the preheated oven for about 30 minutes, or until lightly golden and tender.

Meanwhile, heat the remaining olive oil in a frying pan. Add the onion and cook for 2–3 minutes until tender but not coloured. Add the garlic and spices and cook for another 2 minutes until golden and fragrant. Add the cherry tomatoes to the pan and continue to cook until they start to soften.

Tip the contents of the pan into the roasting dish with the potatoes, season with salt and black pepper, stir to combine and return to the oven for another 5 minutes.

Serve warm, garnished with the chopped parsley.

You can use leftover risotto for these rice balls if you happen to have any, but as they are so delicious it's worth making the risotto especially. They can be prepared and rolled in advance; coat them in breadcrumbs and fry just before serving.

arancini
with pecorino, porcini & mozzarella

15 g/½ oz. dried porcini mushrooms

1 tablespoon olive oil

2 tablespoons unsalted butter

2 shallots, finely chopped

1 fat garlic clove, crushed

250 g/1¼ cups risotto rice (arborio or carnaroli)

750–850 ml/3–3½ cups hot vegetable stock

40 g/⅓ cup grated Pecorino

1 tablespoon freshly chopped flat-leaf parsley or oregano

125 g/4 oz. mozzarella, diced

100 g/¾ cup plain/all-purpose flour

2 eggs, lightly beaten

200 g/2 cups fresh, fine breadcrumbs

about 1 litre/4 cups sunflower oil, for frying

sea salt and freshly ground black pepper

makes 15–18

Soak the porcini in a small bowl of boiling water for about 15 minutes, or until soft. Drain well on kitchen paper/paper towels and finely chop.

Heat the olive oil and butter in a medium saucepan and add the shallots, garlic and chopped porcini. Cook over low–medium heat until soft but not coloured. Add the rice to the pan and stir to coat well in the buttery mixture. Gradually add the vegetable stock – add it one ladleful at a time, and as the stock is absorbed by the rice, add another ladleful, stirring as you do so. Continue cooking in this way until the rice is al dente and the stock is used up. Remove the pan from the heat, add the pecorino and herbs and season well with salt and black pepper. Tip the risotto into a bowl and let cool completely.

Once the rice is cold, divide it into walnut-sized pieces and roll into balls. Taking one ball at a time, flatten it into a disc in the palm of your hand, press some diced mozzarella in the middle and wrap the rice around it to completely encase the cheese. Shape into a neat ball. Repeat with the remaining risotto.

Tip the flour, beaten eggs and breadcrumbs into separate shallow bowls. Roll the rice balls first in the flour, then coat well in the eggs and finally, roll them in the breadcrumbs to completely coat.

Fill a deep-fat fryer with sunflower oil or pour oil to a depth of about 5 cm/2 inches into a deep saucepan. Heat until a cube of bread sizzles and browns in about 5 seconds. Cook the arancini, in batches, in the hot oil for 3–4 minutes or until crisp, hot and golden brown. Drain on kitchen paper/paper towels.

Focaccia is one of the tastiest breads to make, and so easy that it's a crime not to bake it yourself. This focaccia can be made in advance and sliced just before serving.

assorted focaccia crostini

500 g/4 cups (strong) white bread flour

7-g sachet/package or 3 level teaspoons fast-action/instant dried yeast

1 teaspoon fine sea salt

4 tablespoons extra virgin olive oil

300 ml/1¼ cups hand-hot water

2 tablespoons fresh rosemary leaves

2 generous teaspoons sea salt flakes

garlic mushrooms

1 tablespoon olive oil

1 tablespoon unsalted butter

1 shallot, finely chopped

250 g/8 oz. mixed wild mushrooms

1 tablespoon freshly chopped flat-leaf parsley

1 garlic clove

mediterranean tomatoes

4 ripe tomatoes

1 roasted red (bell) pepper, from a jar

1 tablespoon fresh basil leaves, torn

1 tablespoon mixed pitted olives, chopped

100 g/3½ oz. buffalo mozzarella, torn

1 garlic clove

beans & mint

175 g/1⅓ cups cooked broad/fava beans and/or peas, crushed

1 tablespoon freshly chopped mint

grated zest of ½ unwaxed lemon

100 g/3½ oz. feta, crumbled

1 garlic clove

baking tin/pan, 20 x 30 cm/8 x 12 in.

serves 4–6

Mix together the flour, yeast and fine salt in a large bowl. Add 1 tablespoon of the olive oil and the water and mix to a soft dough. Lightly dust the work surface with flour, tip the dough out of the bowl and knead for 10 minutes, or until smooth and elastic. Shape the dough into a neat, smooth ball, return to the bowl and cover with clingfilm/plastic wrap. Leave in a warm place for 1 hour, or until doubled in size. Lightly oil the baking tin/pan. Dust the work surface with flour, tip the dough out and knead for 30 seconds. Roll the dough into a rectangle to fit in the baking tin/pan. Lay the dough inside the tin/pan. Cover with oiled clingfilm/plastic wrap and leave in a warm place for about 1 hour, or until doubled in size. Preheat the oven to 220°C (425°F) Gas 7. Dimple the surface of the dough with your fingertips, drizzle the remaining olive oil all over it and scatter the rosemary and salt flakes over the top. Bake in the preheated oven for about 20 minutes, or until golden brown and well risen. Let cool in the tin/pan for about 10 minutes, then transfer to a wire rack. Cut the focaccia into finger-width slices, toast both sides on a ridged stovetop griddle/grill pan and top with one of the following toppings.

For garlic mushrooms, heat the oil and butter in a frying pan, add the shallot and cook over medium heat until translucent. Add the mushrooms, season, cook until tender and stir through the parsley. Rub the garlic clove over the toasted bread and pile the mixture on top. Drizzle with olive oil. Serve warm.

For Mediterranean tomatoes, chop the tomatoes and red pepper. Add the basil and olives and gently stir through the mozzarella. Rub the garlic clove over the toasted bread and pile the mixture on top. Drizzle with olive oil. Serve hot.

For beans & mint, cook the beans in lightly salted boiling water until tender. Drain and refresh under cold water. Drain well, then whiz in a food processor to a coarse purée. Stir in the mint, lemon and feta and season. Rub the garlic clove over the toasted bread and pile the mixture on top. Drizzle with olive oil. Serve hot.

Grated carrot and courgette/zucchini are bound together here in a spicy, chickpea-flour batter. Chickpea flour (also called gram flour or besan) is available in health food or Asian food stores, but if you can't find it, use plain/all-purpose flour instead.

carrot & chickpea pancakes
with hummus & slow-roasted tomatoes

8–10 tomatoes

2 tablespoons olive oil

1 sprig of fresh thyme

1 tub of hummus

2 handfuls of baby salad leaves or sprouting seeds, such as alfalfa and radish

fruity extra virgin olive oil, for drizzling

carrot & chickpea pancakes

125 g/1 scant cup coarsely grated courgette/zucchini

125 g/1 cup coarsely grated carrot

1 garlic clove, crushed

1 tablespoon freshly chopped coriander/cilantro

1 tablespoon freshly chopped mint

½ teaspoon ground cumin

½ teaspoon ground coriander

¼ teaspoon ground cayenne pepper

125 g/1 cup chickpea flour or plain/all-purpose flour

½ teaspoon baking powder

100 g/3½ oz. feta, crumbled

100 ml/½ cup milk

1 egg, lightly beaten

sea salt and freshly ground black pepper

1 tablespoon sunflower oil

makes 12–15 pancakes

Preheat the oven to 170°C (325°F) Gas 3.

Cut the tomatoes in half, arrange on a small baking sheet, cut-side up, and drizzle the olive oil over them. Scatter the leaves from the thyme all over the top and season with salt and black pepper. Roast on the middle shelf of the preheated oven for 30–40 minutes until soft and starting to brown at the edges. Remove from the oven and let cool to room temperature.

To make the carrot & chickpea pancakes, tip the grated courgette/zucchini, carrot, garlic, herbs, spices, flour and baking powder into a mixing bowl and stir until combined. Add the feta, milk and egg and mix into a batter. Season the mixture well with salt and black pepper.

Heat half the sunflower oil in a frying pan. Add 4 tablespoons of the batter to the pan in separate dollops. Cook over low–medium heat for about 2 minutes, or until golden brown on the underside. Carefully flip the pancakes over and cook the other side until golden. Remove from the pan and keep warm while you cook the remaining batter, adding more oil to the pan as and when needed.

To serve, arrange the pancakes on plates with hummus, the slow-roasted tomatoes and baby salad leaves, drizzle olive oil over the top and serve warm.

I love the squeaky texture of hot, salty halloumi cheese. Serve these vibrant skewers with warm flatbreads or pita breads and a good spoonful of the herby tapenade. The skewers can be prepared in advance but should be eaten immediately after cooking.

chargrilled halloumi
with mixed olive & herb tapenade

250 g/8 oz. halloumi
1 red (bell) pepper, seeds removed
1 courgette/zucchini
1 teaspoon coriander seeds
1 teaspoon cumin seeds
1 garlic clove, crushed
½ teaspoon dried oregano
2–3 tablespoons olive oil
sea salt and freshly ground black pepper
toasted flatbreads or pita breads, to serve

tapenade
4 tablespoons mixed pitted olives
½ small preserved lemon, rind only
2 tablespoons fresh flat-leaf parsley leaves
1 tablespoon fresh mint leaves
1 garlic clove
4 tablespoons fruity extra virgin olive oil

8 wooden skewers

serves 4

Cut the halloumi into chunks and place in a shallow dish. Cut the red pepper and courgette/zucchini into chunks the same size as the halloumi and add to the shallow dish.

Toast the coriander seeds and cumin seeds in a dry frying pan over medium heat for about 1 minute, or until aromatic. Crush lightly using a pestle and mortar and add to the halloumi and vegetables. Add the garlic, oregano and olive oil. Season with black pepper, mix well to combine and set aside to marinate for an hour or so. Meanwhile, soak the wooden skewers in water so that they don't burn when you cook them.

To make the tapenade, tip all the ingredients into a food processor and whiz until combined and roughly chopped. Taste and add black pepper and salt if necessary, but remember that the halloumi is quite salty already.

Preheat a ridged stovetop griddle/grill pan. Thread the marinated halloumi, courgettes/zucchini and peppers onto the wooden skewers, making sure that each one has an even amount of vegetables and cheese. Cook the skewers in the hot pan in batches until golden and the cheese has softened. Serve with the tapenade and toasted flatbreads or pita breads.

index